Getting the Most Out of Web-Based Surveys

By David Ward

American Library Association
Chicago 2000

LITA Guides
#6

ISBN 0-8389-8108-9

Printed in the United States of America

Table of Contents

Introduction

Librarians traditionally have used surveys as a means of gathering input from a variety of diverse groups. Surveys can help evaluate user services, rate different library programs, conduct needs assessments, aid faculty research, and more. The popularity of surveys in the current library environment is evidenced by a simple search of "survey or surveys" on Library Literature – over 5,000 hits at the end of 1999. In the Internet age, posting surveys to the Web provides an easy and convenient way to reach intended audiences, centralizes data collection, and can potentially give librarians far greater control over analyzing and reporting results. Creating Web surveys themselves can be a fairly straight-forward process for those with HTML skills, but the stumbling block for many comes on the "back-end" of Web-based surveys. Once the surveys are submitted, gathering all of the data into a comprehensible whole that can be manipulated, tabulated, and processed into clean reports is a daunting task. This guide will show beginning and advanced users how to create robust Web-based surveys, and then gather their data into a compact and easy to use format.

Library growth and development depend upon responsiveness to patrons' perceived needs. Surveys can help evaluate many types of public services, including instruction workshops, reference services, quality of physical facilities, online and paper resources, as well as more intangible quantities such as perceived helpfulness and usefulness of the library itself. Examples of possible types include user surveys, faculty research (instead of getting emails from LISTSERV queries), needs assessment, and gathering feedback of any sort from a specific population.

We will show you the nuts and bolts for the development and use of such Web-based surveys. The basic premise is to take the data collected by a survey and turn it into a plain text file, which can then be imported into common productivity software programs (like database and spreadsheet applications) and analyzed. In the first step of this process, you will be asked to conceptualize what sort of data you want to gather, and how you intend to use it afterwards. Next, you will need to construct a Web page to gather user input. Instructions will be provided about the design and coding of that page. Then you will modify a generic back-end PERL script to process this data. The script will write each survey response into a plain text file, which you can then import into databases, spreadsheets, and other applications. Finally, you will learn what you can do with all of this information once it is safe and sound in the application of your choice.

It should be noted that there are many other ways to produce the end result we are looking for – survey data in a compact and portable form. However, other methods (like using Microsoft ASP pages and VBscript to write directly to Access/SQL databases, for example) require more programming knowledge, and can be overly restrictive in their application. Our idea is to design a process that can easily be used in a variety of environments.

Chapter 1
Background

System Requirements

The methods described have been tested for UNIX, LINUX, and Windows NT environments. Implementation differences will be discussed in the appropriate sections below. This paper also assumes use of some form of software (database, spreadsheet, etc.) that allows importing text files. Microsoft Office products will be used in the examples, although other database and productivity software should be able to use the data gathered.

Technical Skills Required

- HTML - A basic knowledge of writing web pages with HTML will be needed – e.g. how to place text and images on a page, how to use paragraphs and line breaks, etc. The tags required for constructing HTML Forms will be shown below.
- Database Experience - We will look specifically at importing survey data into Microsoft Access databases. Familiarity with Access is useful, although the techniques taught can be used for other software. While one need not be an expert in databases to use these techniques, some familiarity with whatever software an individual has access to will be helpful.
- PERL - While useful, no Perl knowledge is required. One basic Perl script will be given in its entirety later, with specific instructions for customizing it for specific surveys.
- UNIX – Basic knowledge of UNIX file editing and FTP procedures is needed if you plan to runs these scripts on a UNIX system. The Perl and HTML files used will need to be placed on the server, and in some circumstances (see "A Final Note on PERL" below) they might need to be edited after this transfer.

Chapter 2
The Front End

Before You Start

The first thing to do when designing a Survey of any kind is to think about what kind of information you want from the survey, and what you want to do with it afterward. Both of these factors will influence how you will go about designing both the user interface and the back end PERL (or other) script to process the data. Some questions to consider:

- What is the goal of the survey?
- Who will be taking the survey?
- How will they find out about the survey?
- Do you want the option for open ended answers and/or comments, or do you want to present only a list of specific choices?
- Do you want demographic information on those taking the survey?
- Who will be viewing the results of the survey?
- What do you want the results of the survey to tell you?
- How do you want to tabulate the results? (charts/graphs, raw numbers, percents, etc.)
- What sorts of reports do you want to make from the results?

There is a large amount of background work that needs to be done before any “scientific” survey is conducted. Going into great detail on measurement methodologies and sampling techniques is not in this work’s scope, but we will recommend a couple of good sources (Powell and Van House) in the Works Consulted section that detail this process.

HTML Forms

An HTML Form allows Web developers to design a graphical interface for gathering information from users. Visually, forms are similar to their paper counterparts - job applications, order forms, etc. The HTML coding for forms is fairly straight-forward. Our main examples use the most basic HTML tags, for simplicity and to speed learning of the process. For those that want to get more in depth, most HTML reference books cover Form coding in detail, and most HTML editors have buttons for easy creation of Form elements. The examples below will display and function in text based browsers like LYNX, but for those interested in creating truly ADA compliant pages, look at the W3C's website on Accessibility under *Recommended Reading*, and the "W3C Accessibility Guidelines Compliant Example" in the Appendix.

Form tags follow the same standard layout as other HTML. It is important that each "element" or "field" (piece of a form) have its own unique "NAME," so that it can be referred to later. To avoid problems later, most NAMEs should be all lower case, and **must not** contain any spaces or slashes (/). For our purposes, it is also important that a default "VALUE" is assigned to each element. Together, these "NAME" and "VALUE" pairs comprise the data that we will be taking from the survey.

Below are descriptions of some of the common FORM elements used in surveys:

FORM tag

```
<FORM ACTION= "/cgi-bin/myscript.pl" METHOD= "post"> </FORM>
```

Creates a form. `<FORM` etc.....>

Must be used before all other tags, and `</FORM>` must be used after all form tags. `ACTION` is the location of the script that will process the form, and `METHOD` is how the data is sent to the script (either "post" or "get"). "Get" submits a form and encodes the elements in the URL, and is read by PERL from the "`QYERY_STRING`" variable. "Post" encodes the elements in the body of the document, and is read by PERL from the variable "`CONTENT_LENGTH`". (See Appendix, Sample PERL Script lines 34-40) The main reason I use `POST` in the example script is because it doesn't display the fields in the URL when the user Submits the form (e.g. with `GET` the user sees :

```
http://myserver.com/cgi-
bin/myscript.pl?first=fred&last=smith etc.)
```

Text Boxes

```
Last Name : <INPUT TYPE= "text" NAME= "last" VALUE= " "
SIZE= "20">
```

Creates a 20 character long text box that any text can be typed into. VALUE can be set to anything, or just “” for a blank space.

Last Name:

Illustration 2.1 Sample Text Field

Check Boxes

```
<INPUT TYPE= "checkbox" NAME= "checkbox1" VALUE= "books"
checked>
```

A check box is a square that is marked with a check mark when the user clicks in it. Any number of checkboxes may be chosen for any given NAME. If groups of checkboxes share the same NAME, they will send multiple VALUES to the PERL script. “Checked” means that an individual checkbox is chosen by default.

☐ Books

Illustration 2.2 Sample Checkbox Field

Radio Buttons

```
<INPUT TYPE= "radio" NAME="radio1" VALUE= "yes" checked>
```

Like checkboxes, except that only one may be chosen for any given NAME. Usually used in “Yes/NO” or “Either/Or” type situations.

Yes ◉ No ○

Illustration 2.3 Sample Radio Button Field

Reset Buttons

```
<INPUT TYPE= "reset" VALUE= "reset the form">
```

Creates a grey button that returns all VALUEs to their default setting on a form. VALUE is the text that appears on the button. This is a standard button pre-defined by HTML.

reset the form!

Illustration 2.4 Sample Reset Button

Submit Buttons

```
<INPUT TYPE= "submit" VALUE= "Send the Survey">
```

Creates a button that sends the form to the script specified above in the "FORM ACTION=" statement. VALUE is the text that appears on the button.

Send the Survey

Illustration 2.5 Sample Submit Button

Text Areas

```
<TEXTAREA NAME= "comments" VALUE= " " COLS=40
ROWS=5></TEXTAREA>
```

Creates a 40 by 5 area in which users can enter text. Value can be set to a default text that would appear in the box. A text area is useful for getting user comments, or any time you want a lengthy reply to a survey question.

Illustration 2.6 Sample Text Area Field

Select field / Pull-Down Boxes

```
<SELECT NAME= "evaluation">
<OPTION VALUE= "4">Very Useful
<OPTION VALUE= "3">Somewhat Useful
<OPTION VALUE= "2">Not Useful
<OPTION VALUE= "1">Rather Watch TV
</SELECT>
```

Creates a pull-down menu of choices, only one of which can be chosen. VALUE is what will be sent to the PERL script when a particular option is chosen.

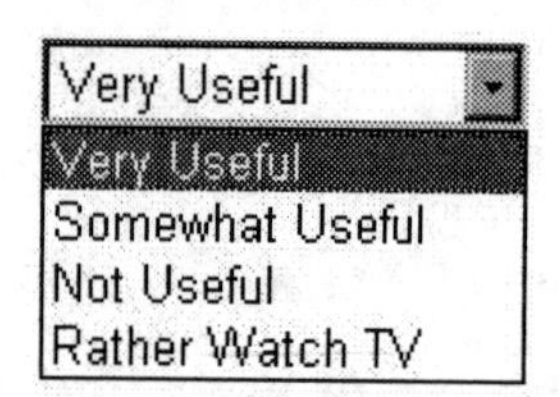

Illustration 2.7 Sample Select Field

More Select Field Options

```
<SELECT multiple NAME= "frequency" size= "2">
<OPTION VALUE= "4">More than once a week
<OPTION VALUE= "3">Weekly
<OPTION VALUE= "2">Monthly
<OPTION VALUE= "1">Less Than Monthly
</SELECT>
```

The same as above, but "multiple" means that more than one choice can be selected (by holding down the CTRL key and clicking on your choices), and "size=2" means two choices are shown initially. Note that the box scrolls with multiple, as opposed to dropping down in the previous example.

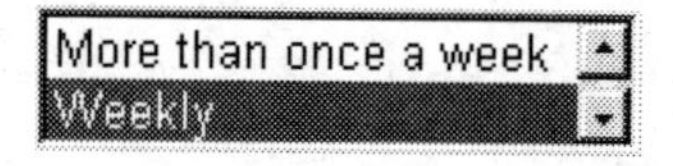

Illustration 2.8 Sample Multiple Select Field

Tips

When you are doing ratings of services, facilities, etc., try assigning numbers as VALUEs in the Form. For example, if the question is : "How often do you find what you need?" And the OPTIONs in a SELECT are "Always, Often, Sometimes, Never", you can assign VALUEs of 4, 3, 2, and 1 instead of the text equivalents. In this way, numbers are gathered which can be used for generating averages, means, etc. later on in a spreadsheet or database that you send the data to. [Van House 1990]

The appendices provide examples of several HTML forms. Appendix A4 is a form to solicit information from faculty members; A5 is a sample student survey regarding Internet use; and the survey in appendix A6 is about library reference use.

Chapter 3
Designing A Database

Once you have designed the form, the next step is to decide which software program you will use to process the data. We will use Microsoft Access as our example, although other databases and spreadsheet programs are equally applicable (see Appendices A8 for an example using EXCEL and A9 for Filemaker Pro). To create a new database, open Access and choose "File>>New Database." Access will prompt you to save the new database. Then click on the "Tables" tab and choose "New". Lastly, choose "Design View" and click ok.

The first step is to look at what data you gather in your form. For each element in the form, we will want a corresponding "field" in our Access table. They should both have the same NAME to facilitate import into the database management program. All of the fields in a single survey response taken together make up a single "record." The VALUE sent from the form for a particular name will (later on) be imported and assigned to the appropriate field. The "Data Type" for each field should correspond to what the form will gather and send to the database program.

The most common types are :

- text – Plain text, up to 255 characters long

  Examples : text boxes, SELECT fields, Check Boxes or Radio Buttons, etc.

- memo – Plain text, no length limit (but not searchable by Access)

  Example : Usually just used with Text areas

- number – A Number

  Example : A Select Field where you are sending numbers as VALUEs

- yes/no – A yes/no or checked/unchecked data type. I usually don't use these when importing data because these VALUES can be given some odd interpretations by database management systems (i.e. giving "yes" and underlying value of -1, and "no" and underlying value of 0). Use text instead, giving the values as "Y" and "N" or something equally obvious.

article : Table

Field Name	Data Type	Description
ID	AutoNumber	
last name	Text	
first name	Text	
student	Text	
before	Text	
frequency	Number	
evaluation	Number	
comments	Memo	

Field Properties

General | Lookup

Field Size	Long Integer
New Values	Increment
Format	
Caption	
Indexed	Yes (No Duplicates)

The field description is optional. It helps you describe the field and is also displayed in the status bar when you select this field on a form. Press F1 for help on descriptions.

Illustration 3.1 Access Table in Design View

When you have finished choosing fields, close the table window. Access will prompt you to save the table, and ask for a name. Next, it will ask you if you want to specify a “Primary ID.” Usually, you should click yes here. A Primary ID is a unique identifier (like a barcode number) that is assigned to each “record.” Unless you are actually gathering patron barcode numbers, it is probably a good idea to just let Access assign an “Auto-Number” field by clicking “Yes.”

!Reminder - The order of the fields will be very important later on, so make a note of them after you are done. Again, you must have a field for every element NAME and VALUE pair you are gathering in the HTML Form.

One last thing you might also want to do is to use the Access Forms wizard to create a more attractive way to look at your data. A normal Access table has fixed-width cells which, while fine for numbers and short names, is cumbersome if you have essay/comment type responses. To create an Access Form, click on the Forms tab, choose New, the Forms Wizard, and specify your table in the drop down box.

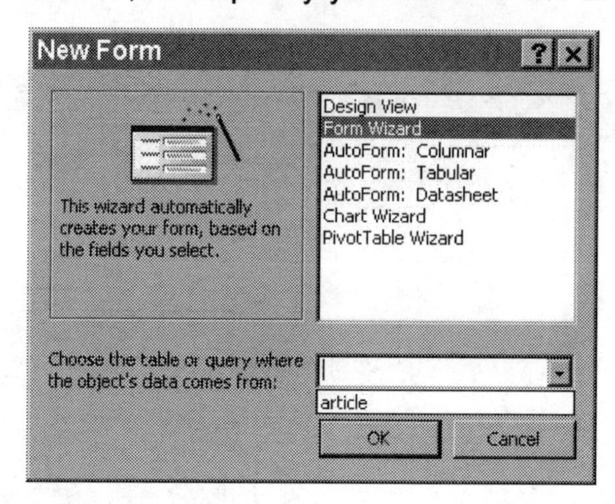

Illustration 3.2 Access Form Creation Dialog Box

Hit "OK" and select all of the fields you want displayed in the following dialog box.

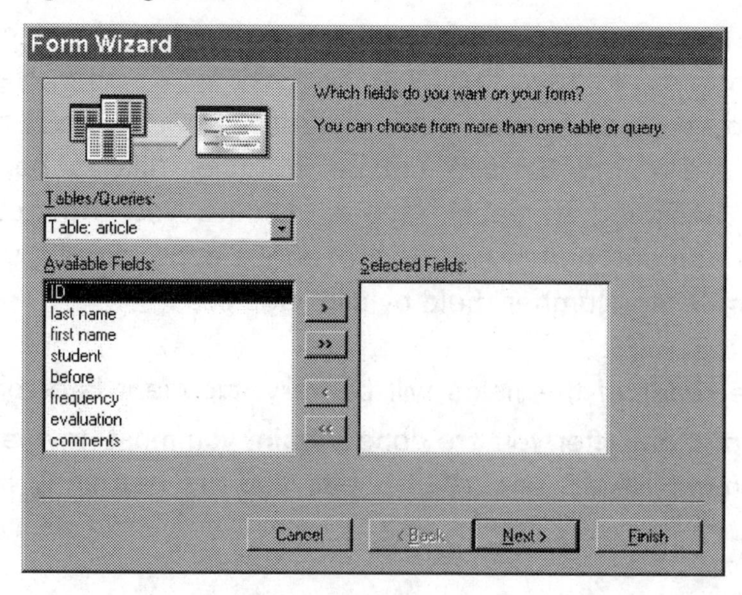

Illustration 3.3 Access Form – Second Dialog Box

The remaining dialog boxes will give you options for appearance and ordering options for the records – these are really up to you. After you are done with the Wizard, open the form in Design view, and drag around the boxes for the essay length fields until they are big enough to see everything. Pretty handy!

article : Form
Form Header
Detail
ID
last name
first name
student
before
frequency
evaluation
comments
Form Footer
Toolbox

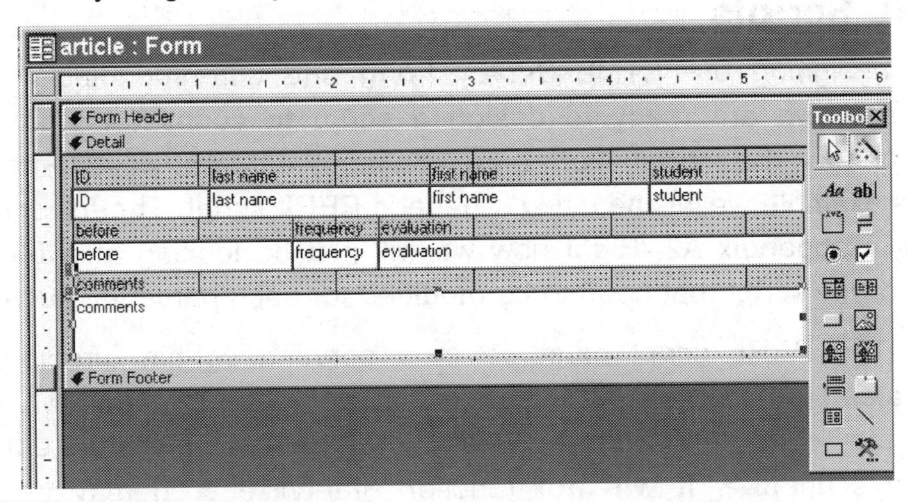

Illustration 3.4 Access Form in Design Mode

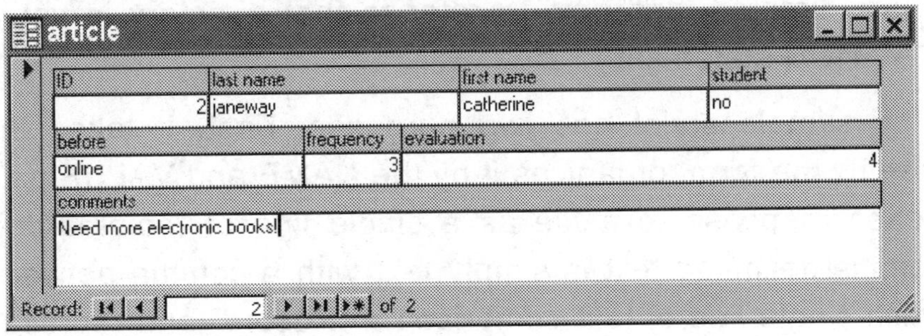

article
ID
last name
first name
student
2
janeway
catherine
no
before
frequency
evaluation
online
3
4
comments
Need more electronic books!
Record:
2
of 2

Illustration 3.5 Access Form in Open Mode

Chapter 4
The Back End

PERL Scripts

After designing our HTML Survey Form and corresponding Access database, we are ready to design a script to connect the two. As mentioned in the Introduction, there are many different ways to do this; in this example we will be using a generic PERL script. The full script is listed in appendix A2. Right now we will just be looking at a few key parts of the script that need to be modified for each particular survey.

The PERL script must be in a server's cgi-bin directory (or equivalent) in order to run. This is usually accessed by the HTML page with the code "<FORM ACTION = "http://www.mylibrary.edu/cgi-bin/my_script.pl">. It **will not** function otherwise. You may need to consult your systems office to see about getting it added to the appropriate directory and how to refer to that directory in your HTML Form's ACTION statement.

The sample script has two purposes. First, it takes the data submitted by the form, organizes it by the NAME and VALUE pairs, and writes each response to a file as a single line of "comma-delimited" text. Comma-delimited text is simply text with a comma between each field. Each single line of text comprises a "Record" and represents the results of one user taking the survey (see appendix A3 for an example).

Example Form and Resulting Text File

Form:

```
First Name: <INPUT TYPE= "Text" NAME= "first" VALUE= "">
<br>
Last Name: <INPUT TYPE= "Text" NAME= "last" VALUE= "">
<br>
Occupation: <INPUT TYPE= "Text" NAME= "occ" VALUE= "">
```

Resulting Comma Delimited Text: (after 3 users submit and PERL script processes)

```
"bill", "clinton", "president"
"cuomo", "mario", "ex-mayor"
"lincoln", "abraham", "in hiding"
```

The second purpose is to provide feedback to the user after they Submit the survey. This is accomplished by embedding HTML within the PERL script, so that after the text file is written, a feedback message can be given. We will look at the relevant parts of the PERL script for both of these purposes below, and explain how to modify them to suit individual needs. If you have a background in PERL, you should feel free to experiment with the PERL code we don't cover as well.

ıNote: Depending on the editor that you use to create your PERL script you may see line numbers at the beginning of each line. Lines proceeded by a # are called "comments" – they don't actually do anything in the PERL script. Deleting the # (or "uncommenting" them) from the lines in our examples will cause PERL to look at the lines and try to do something with them. This will probably cause an error in your program.

File Location

The first part to modify is the location to which we will be writing the plain text file, and the file's name. The following lines of code cover this:

```
# file sharing variables

# $EXCLUSIVE_LOCK = 2;
# $UNLOCK = 8;
  $PATH = "";          # path to directory where file will be
          writen (default is cgi-bin)
$REPORT_FILE = "report.txt";          # file to append test
          results
$REPORT = $PATH . $REPORT_FILE;       # must build file and
                                    # directory path separately
```

The first two variables ($EXCLUSIVE_LOCK and $UNLOCK) are optional. They are used later on to make sure that only one person can write to the text file at a time, to avoid strange errors. Usually you will want to uncomment them (remove the #), but some PERL systems will balk at that, so I have left them commented to get started.

$PATH is the actual directory where the file will be. Since the PERL script resides in the cgi-bin directory, a blank value means PERL will try to write the file to "cgi-bin". This is usually not a good idea, so consult with your systems people to find an appropriate and secure directory to write the file to. $REPORT_FILE is the name of the text file itself. $REPORT puts these together :

Example of Specifying a Path and Filename

Here is a sample directory structure :

```
/root
|
  -- cgi-bin
|
  -- users
      -- david
```

If I want to call my file "david_survey.txt", and store it in my directory under "users/david", I would use the following values for my variables :

```
$PATH = "../users/david/";
# the two dots (..) represent going up one directory - to root
$REPORT_FILE = "david_survey.txt";
```

HTML Feedback

The feedback the user gets after submitting the form is generated by placing regular HTML between certain print statements, as below :

In the example in the Appendix, you can see that it is also possible to include data from the form in the feedback. This is done by using the structure $FORM{'name_of_form_element'}, where 'name_of_form_element' refers to the NAME we assigned to an element of the HTML Form (see above). Any HTML can be included in this part, including Javascript and DHTML elements. Generally it is advisable to keep it simple, and to provide a link back to the regular library page. The text you type in here is not subject to the normal strict rules for PERL (like text or line wrapping - see *Testing Phase*), although if you type in invalid HTML, the feedback page will not display correctly.

Example HTML Feedback in PERL script

```
print "Content-type: text/html\n\n";
print <<_END_OF_HTML;

<h2>Form Successfully Completed!</h2>
$FORM{'first'}, we value your comments!<br>

<a href= "myserver.edu/homepage.html">Click Here</a> to go
back to our homepage!</a>

_END_OF_HTML
```

Writing the Text File

At this point, you will want to consult the database we created earlier. In the final section of code, we need to tell PERL in what order to write the fields from the Form to the text file, and this needs to correspond to the order we want it to appear in the database. The following lines of code accomplish this:

The array @fields (Line 142 in the example script) is a list of all but one of the NAMEs from the elements in our HTML Form, in the order that you have the corresponding Access fields listed in your table (from Chapter 3). However, the last field in the Access table should not be in the array @fields, but rather addressed after this, on Line 152. This is because of the way data is imported into most programs : the last field should have no comma after it, and a new line or hard return (like pressing the enter key) after it. All of the other fields are written to the file with double quotes around them, a comma in between (Lines 145-151),+ and no hard return.

I would like to stress again that the fields you send here must match exactly the fields you will be using in Access (or whatever program you will be importing to). This means if you have 5 data elements (fields) in your Form, the PERL program needs to receive 5 NAME and VALUE pairs, even if some VALUEs are null (""). The reason is that when Form data is sent to a script for processing, if no default value is assigned and the user leaves a field blank, PERL will not receive a NAME and VALUE pair for that field – i.e., it will be as if that field doesn't exist, which could really muddle things up when you try to import the data later.

One other function the PERL script performs when writing to the text file is to eliminate all commas and double quote marks (lines 147-148) from each field. Earlier in the script (lines 57-58), we also eliminated all hard returns from the data. This is to prevent errors in importing later, because all of these characters are treated in a special way during the importing process.

Test the Form and Script

There are a few areas for potential error in this entire process. Before implementing your HTML pages and PERL scripts, it is a good idea to test them first. If you wish to test your survey on your desktop, there are many free server software programs out there that will emulate the web server environment on your PC. I recommend Xitami (see Recommended Reading) which is easy to implement and has easy to use features for testing scripts. Fill in your form and submit it a few times (a shortcut is to fill it in once and hit your Browser's reload button after you submit it). Make sure to try all of the possible error conditions (your users will find them if you don't).

If your browser gives you errors upon submitting the FORM, review the guidelines above and check the section below for some common errors. Otherwise, check in the directory where you were writing the text file to see if it is there and that the content appears as comma-delimited text. If not, you'll need to debug your PERL program (see under "Syntax errors," below).

Once you are able to fill out the form and see the correct results in the output file you can proceed to the section on *Importing Data* to process your FORM results.

Below are some of the common types of errors you should check for if you get error messages when testing :

Syntax errors : Otherwise known as spelling errors or typing errors. These can occur in both the HTML and PERL pages, but have different effects on both. HTML is very forgiving, so if you make a spelling error (such as name= “frist” instead of name= “first”) it will generally ignore it or try to compose the rest of the page around the error. If your page as displayed in a browser ever looks odd or is formatted/centered differently from what you expected, check for syntax errors in the HTML itself.

Example (missing quotation mark in href):

```
<a href= "home_page.html>Home Page</a>
<br>
Hello Patron!
```

This could result in “Hello Patron” becoming a link, or it could just not appear on the page, depending upon which browser you use and how it interprets the HTML.

PERL scripts aren’t nearly as forgiving as HTML. You must have a semicolon (;) at the end of every line. Also, you can’t wrap lines of

PERL code like you can HTML – a single command or statement that runs across multiple line will be treated as multiple command, usually generating errors. If you misspell a word, or leave out a quotation mark or a parenthesis, most of the time the script will not execute and will return an error message. Unfortunately, most error messages for PERL display the same message in the browser, so you generally need to look at the script line by line to see where the error is. One way around this is to use the built-in PERL debugger that runs on UNIX, and also comes with Active State PERL for Windows (see Appendix). To use this debugger, go to a UNIX or DOS prompt, change to the directory your script is in, and type "perl –d my_script.pl". The debugger will run through the script one line at a time (type "n" to go to the next line), and stop when it gets to a line with some problems. The debugger isn't perfect, but it can give you a good idea of where to start looking for errors.

Example of a PERL syntax error (missing quotation mark and misspelled field name):

```
@fields = {"last", "frist", "age, "occupation"};
```

Example of a PERL syntax error (wrapped lines):

```
@fields = {"last", "first", "age", "occupation",
"dateofbirth", "taxid", "librarynumber"};
```

This latter statement will generate errors on both lines, and cause PERL to not execute the whole script.

Variable Errors : Because we are matching data elements across many different scripts, software, and files, it is vital that each data element be referred to in a consistent way. Make sure that the "name" of an HTML FORM element is the same as the corresponding entry in the @fields used in PERL. Also, capitalization must remain consistent – if a FORM element has the

NAME "Occupation", then in the PERL @fields it must also be referred to as "Occupation." This will also be covered under the *Importing Data* section below.

Other FORM Errors : Because of the way PERL interprets the data passed to it by the HTML FORM, do NOT include spaces or slashes in a FORM NAME attribute. This can cause unpredictable, and generally undesirable, results.

Example of incorrect naming in an HTML FORM :

```
First Name : <INPUT TYPE= "Text" NAME= "first name">
```

Better Version:

```
First Name : <INPUT TYPE= "Text" NAME= "firstname">
```

Security

The annotated PERL script in the appendix highlights some of the lines of code that deal with security issues. Whenever you run a script, there are possibilities that you are opening your system up to hackers. This script has some built in protections, but there are numerous ways that clever people could try to abuse any HTML form processing script to further their own agenda. For our purposes, the most important thing to consider is to what directory you will be writing the comma delimited text file. This is because the directory to which you write it obviously must have its permissions set in such a way that it can be written to. And here the possibility arises that others might try to write their own programs or files into this directory. Hence, your local systems staff will need to be consulted to find an appropriate location on your system that is protected in such a way that it does not expose your system to intruders.

The default directory ($PATH) we are writing to (the cgi-bin directory) is not the one you ultimately want to use. This might be fine for testing purposes on your own secure system, but you will need to change it when you "go live" because of the considerations above. One solution is a program called "Cgiwrap" that you can ask your systems staff to consider installing on the server (see Resources section). This program allows you to run PERL from your own UNIX account, which serves the double purpose of being isolated enough from the main server, and allowing you to make changes to the PERL script and update it yourself without having to rely on a system administrator to install each of your script changes.

A Final Note on PERL

Because of the eccentricities of the different operating systems, a PERL program written in a PC text editor like Notepad or an HTML editor may not be recognized by UNIX, or LINUX, or whatever is running your server. This seems to stem from the way that certain software encodes line breaks or hard returns. It is important to start with an editor that doesn't automatically wrap lines of text. Notepad and most HTML editors can be configured to turn off line wrapping. Then you can copy and paste the text into an editor on the server (like PICO or EMACS for UNIX) and then save it from that editor. Don't ask me why this works, just live it and breathe it. You should also be able to FTP your PC file to the UNIX machine if FTP is available. If this doesn't work, you might need to hand code your PERL script using a built-in editor like PICO directly on the server.

For example, let's say I have the file my_sricpt.pl on a UNIX server, and it is giving weird error messages when I use it. I can go to the directory it is in, type "pico my_script.pl", then hit ctrl-o (write out) to save it. Magically, when I use Netscape to look at the file again, it works perfectly (assuming there aren't any actual errors in the PERL script itself). Strange things like this are why most of us are librarians and not programmers.

Another thing you will need to do if you are using PERL on a UNIX based machine is to make it accessible to the outside world once you have FTP'ed it (or copied it) to a file in the UNIX machine's cgi-bin directory. The way to do this is with the command "chmod", which stands for "change mode." You (or your systems person) must be in the cgi-bin directory where your script resides, and at the UNIX prompt type "chmod 755 my_script.pl" (substituting the name of your PERL script). This will make the script executable on the Internet – by default, a newly created/transferred script is usually not accessible and will generate an error message in your browser when you submit your HTML form.

Chapter 5
Importing Data

Overview

Now that we have the data in a plain text file, the next step is to put it into a program that can analyze and manipulate it. Again, we are using Microsoft Access as our example, but almost any database software should be able to import comma delimited text and dump it into a table. If your survey involves a lot of numbers – for example, if people are rating services on a scale and you want to do calculations on the average and the mean, etc. – you might want to consider a spreadsheet application with built in mathematical functions (like Excel) as well. (By the way, I'm not trying to hawk Microsoft products, I just find them common enough to be models for this procedure).

First, we need to have a copy of the comma-delimited file our PERL script has created on your computer's local hard drive. If you have it stored on a remote UNIX system, you will need to FTP it from it's location; if you are on a Windows NT or similar network, you will need to copy it to a local directory (i.e. c:\my_survey\) using Windows Explorer, or its equivalent.

The next step is to open the database we created earlier. At this point, it is critical that every line of text in the file you are importing have exactly the same number of fields as the database – see the end of chapter 4 for the specifics on this. If you choose File>>Get External Data>>Import, you will get a dialog box asking for you to choose a file. On the Files of Type dropdown menu (located in the bottom left corner), choose Text. Go to the directory where your text file (report.txt in our example) is located, and choose it.

Import
Look in: cgi-bin
survey
report.txt
Import
Cancel
Advanced...
Find files that match these search criteria:
File name:
Text or property:
Find Now
Files of type: Text Files (*.txt;*.csv;*.tab;*.asc)
Last modified: any time
New Search
Not all file types are installed by default. To add other file types, run the Setup program, click Add/Remove, Data Access, Change Option. Additional file types are also available in the Office 97 ValuPack.
1 file(s) found.

Illustration 5.1 Access Import Dialog Box

The first dialog box asks you to choose the format for the data. Delimited should be chosen – if not, then check it.

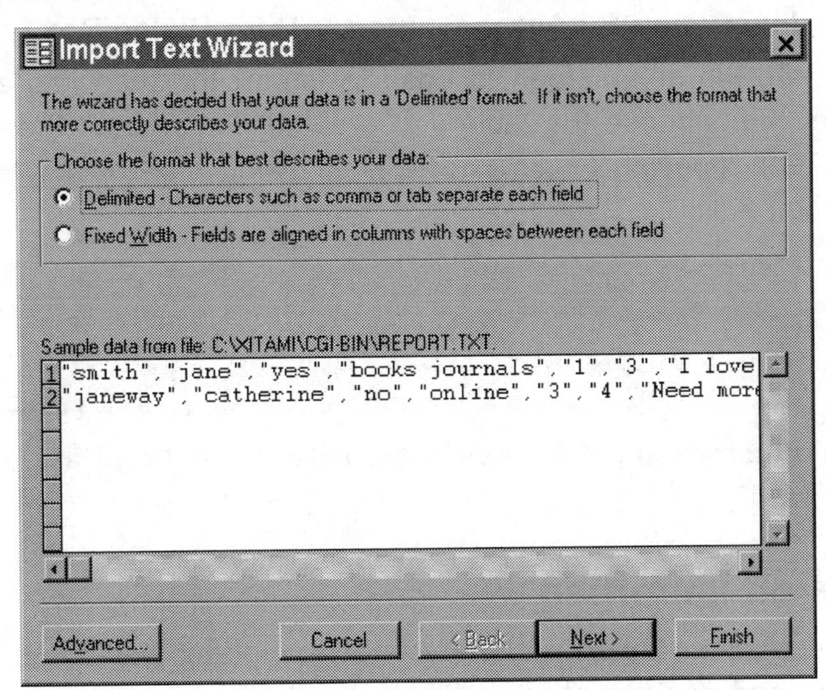

Illustration 5.2 Access Import – Second Dialog Box

Choose Next. You will then be asked to choose the delimiter – Comma, in our case. Make sure this is checked, and that the space for Text Qualifier has a double quote in it (").

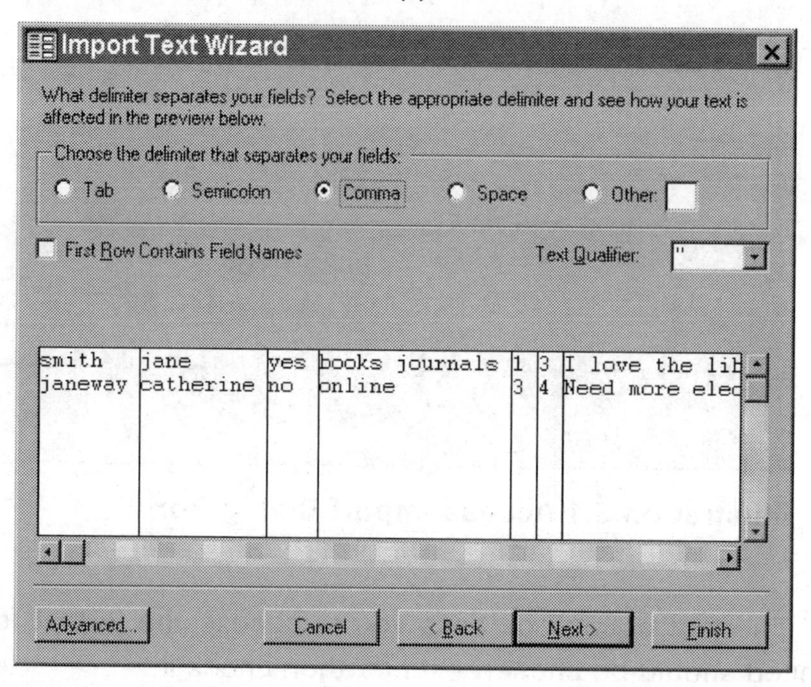

Illustration 5.3 Access Import – Third Dialog Box

On the next screen, choose to import the data into an Existing Table, then choose the table you created earlier from the drop down list. After choosing Finish on the final dialog box, open your table to see the results!

article : Table

ID	last name	first name	student	before	frequency	evaluation	co
1	smith	jane	yes	books journals	1	3	I love
2	janeway	catherine	no	online	3	4	Neec
(AutoNumber)					0	0	

Illustration 5.4 Access Table After Importing Data

Tips on Importing

If you plan to import several times throughout the duration of your survey and don't want to duplicate the same records every time you import, there are a few things you will want to do. Whenever you copy the comma-delimited file from the server to your local drive, make a copy with a new name on the server (e.g. "backup1.txt"), and then delete the original text file from the server. The PERL program will start a new file the next time it gets a response, with the same name specified in the PERL script (e.g. "report.txt"), and you can use your copy for importing purposes.

If you are having problems importing data, or are getting weird results, try importing into a new table. This will often show you the cause of the problem – usually, one "record" or more (equivalent to a line of text in our case) will have either too many or too few fields. This is usually a sign that your HTML Form doesn't have default VALUEs assigned for all of its elements.

The other common problem is in the PERL script. The thing to check here is the array @fields. Make sure it has all but one of the NAMEs from the HTML Form, listed in the order of the Fields in the Access table you will be importing into. Again, the element that will be in the last field of the Access table should be listed separately, on Line 148 in the example. Thus, if you have 5 fields (plus your index, if you created one) in your Access table, the PERL script should have the first four fields (in order) listed in @fields, with the last field on line 148.

Chapter 6
Conclusion

Benefits

There are, as we noted in the introduction, many other ways to accomplish this task. The idea behind creating a comma delimited file from our HTML form is so that you, the librarian, will have a simple and portable format to move your data between applications. This allows for flexibility, and you can use the same PERL script over and over (by changing the appropriate fields and file names) for many different kinds of surveys. Receiving a hundred emails from a LISTSERV query can sometimes be more tedious and time consuming than it is really worth. It is much easier to post a URL and let technology do the hard work for you. Additionally, this method requires a minimum amount of hardcore programming knowledge in order to produce robust results. Once you have done this successfully for one survey, it is easy to do it again and again in other situations.

Gathering user and peer feedback will continue to be of vital importance as technology and the complexities of library services continue to grow. For the librarian, streamlining the mechanical aspects of data collection allows for more quality time in data analysis. This, ultimately, can lead to more productivity, and launching new surveys when circumstances call for it will seem more inviting.

Works Consulted / Recommended Reading

Adams, Mignon S. and Jeffrey A. Beck. *User Surveys in College Libraries.* Chicago : ACRL. 1995.

A collection of sample user surveys.

Brekke, Elaine. *User Surveys in ARL Libraries* (SPEC Kit #205). Washington, D.C. : ARL. 1994.

Has sample surveys like Adams, but also includes sample Results, Analysis, and Methodology of specific surveys.

Powell, Ronald R. Basic *Research Methods for Librarians* (3d ed.) Greenwhich, Connecticut : Ablex Publishing Corporation. 1997.

Powell has in depth chapters on "Survey Research and Sampling" and "Data Collection Techniques," which covers types of questions, etc. Very useful for the designing stage of surveys.

Van House, Nancy A. Beth T. Weil and Charles R. McClure. *Academic Library Performance: A Practical Approach.* Chicago : ALA. 1990.

Talks about methodology and the preparation of user surveys, in addition to coverage of other types of service measurments.

W3C Consortium, "Techniques for Web Content Accessibility Guidelines 1.0"

http://www.w3.org/TR/WAI-WEBCONTENT-TECHS/#forms

Lists the W3C's ADA guidelines for most types of HTML tags. The URL above goes to the section on FORMS and ADA.

Resources

HTML Forms — Any quality reference book on HTML will tell you more about HTML Forms, and how to code the various types of user input elements. There are also many Web-based tutorials, including Webmonkey (http://hotwired.lycos.com/webmonkey/99/30/index4a.html)

CGIWRAP — an explanation of this and instructions for downloading and installing it can be found at : http://www.unixtools.org/cgiwrap/ .

XITAMI — (http://www.imatix.com/html/xitami/index.htm). Free server software that you can run from Windows to test your form and PERL scripts with. It has it's own cgi-bin and PERL support. You should install **ActivePerl** for Windows from the ActiveState site (http://www.activestate.com/) first, so that Windows and Xitami know what to do with your script.

PERL — *Learning Perl, 2d Edition* by Randal L. Schwartz, et al (ISBN 1565922840) is a great intro to the Perl language, and will also help those who want to make more advanced PERL scripts.

Appendices

A1. HTML Form Code

```
<HTML>
<HEAD>
<TITLE>Sample HTML Form</TITLE>
</HEAD>
<BODY>
<CENTER>
<H3>University of LITA Library Survey Form</H3>
Take it now and win cash prizes!
<hr>
</CENTER>

<FORM ACTION="/cgi-bin/my_script.pl" METHOD="post">
Last Name:<INPUT TYPE="text" NAME="last_name" VALUE="">
First Name:<INPUT TYPE="text" NAME="first_name" VALUE="">
<br>
Are you a ULITA student?
Yes<INPUT TYPE="radio" NAME="student" VALUE="yes" checked>
No<INPUT TYPE="radio" NAME="student" VALUE="no">
<br>
Check all the following you have used in the library:
<INPUT TYPE="checkbox" NAME="before" VALUE="books">Books
<INPUT TYPE="checkbox" NAME="before" VALUE="journals">Journals
<INPUT TYPE="checkbox" NAME="before" VALUE="online">Online Resources
<INPUT TYPE="checkbox" NAME="before" VALUE="staff">Staff
<br>
I come to the library:
<SELECT multiple NAME="frequency" size="2">
<OPTION VALUE=4>More than once a week
<OPTION VALUE=3 selected>Weekly
<OPTION VALUE=2>Monthly
<OPTION VALUE=1>Less than Monthly
</SELECT>
<br>
I think overall the library is:
<SELECT NAME="evaluation">
<OPTION VALUE=4>Very Useful
<OPTION VALUE=3>Somewhat Useful
<OPTION VALUE=2>Not Useful
<OPTION VALUE=1>Rather Watch TV
</SELECT>
<br>
Comments:
<br>
<TEXTAREA NAME="comments" VALUE="" COLS="40" ROWS="5"></TEXTAREA>
<br>
<INPUT TYPE="reset" VALUE="reset the form!">
<br>
<INPUT TYPE="submit" VALUE="Submit the Form">

</FORM>
<hr>
</BODY>
</HTML>
```

Screen Shot of Example HTML Form :

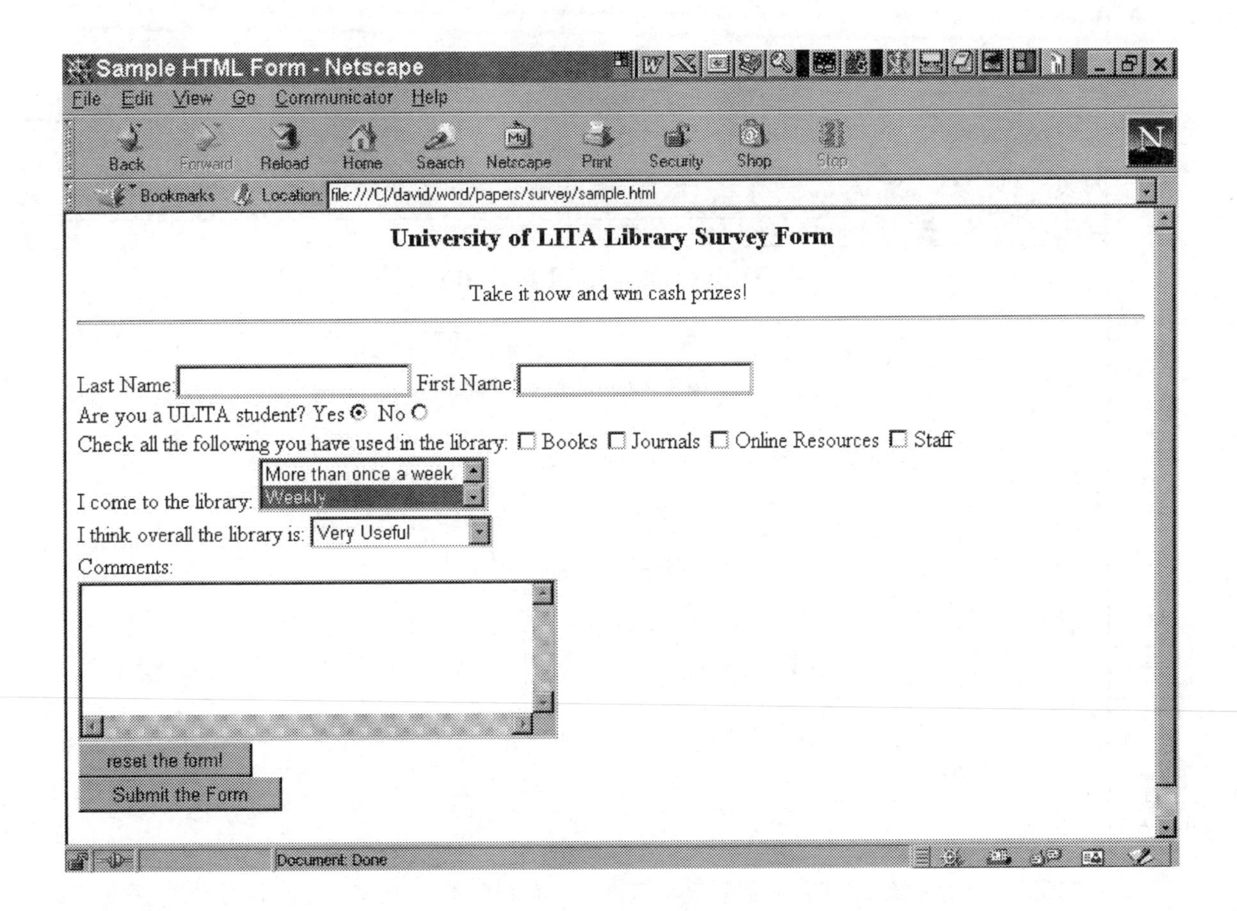

Screenshot of HTML Feedback From PERL script

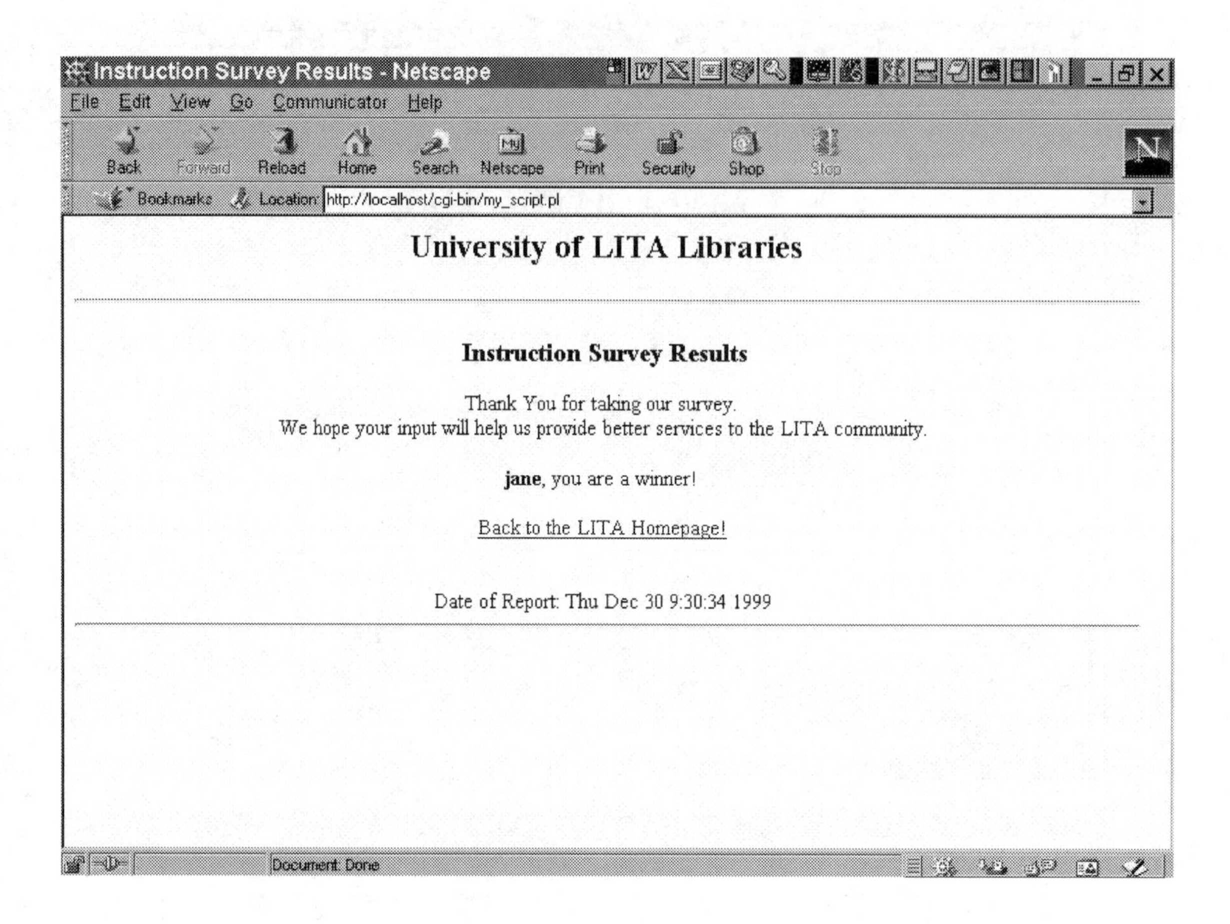

A2. Generic PERL Script

(line numbers listed on the side are not part of the actual code)

```
#!/usr/bin/perl

#
# Library Survey Processing Script
#

require "ctime.pl";       # gets local time

#
# Global Variables
#

%FORM = ();                        # data structure for HTML form

# file sharing variables

# $EXCLUSIVE_LOCK = 2;
# $UNLOCK = 8;
$PATH = "";         # path of webuser home account
$REPORT_FILE = "report.txt";          # file to append test results
$REPORT = $PATH . $REPORT_FILE;       # must build file and directory
path
# separately

# boolean variables

$DATE = &ctime(time);                 # date and time when script is
executed
$TIMESTAMP = "Date of Report: " . $DATE;     # if we want to date each
#  response

#  The next sequence gets the data submitted by the form
#  and turns it into NAME and VALUE pairs in the array %FORM.
#  So, $FORM{'student'} equals the VALUE of the student field from the
form

if ($ENV{'REQUEST_METHOD'} eq 'GET') {
      @pairs = split(/&/, $ENV{'QUERY_STRING'});
}
elsif ($ENV{'REQUEST_METHOD'} eq 'POST') {
      read(STDIN, $buffer, $ENV{'CONTENT_LENGTH'});
      @pairs = split(/&/, $buffer);
}
else {
      $Error_Message = "Bad request method ($ENV{'REQUEST_METHOD'}).";
}

foreach $pair (@pairs) {
      ($name, $value) = split(/=/, $pair);

      $name =~ tr/+/ /;
      $name =~ s/%([a-fA-F0-9][a-fA-F0-9])/pack("C", hex($1))/eg;
      $name =~ s/\n//g;
```

```
        $name =~ s/\r//g;
          $name =~ s/<!--(.|\n)*-->//g;          # check for SSI
          $name =~ /^([-\@\w.]+)$/;              # check for tainted data

        $value =~ tr/+/ /;
        $value =~ s/%([a-fA-F0-9][a-fA-F0-9])/pack("C", hex($1))/eg;
        $value =~ s/\n//g;
        $value =~ s/\r//g;
        $value =~ s/<!--(.|\n)*-->//g;           # security : check for SSI
        $value =~ /^([-\@\w.]+)$/;               # security : check for
tainted data

        if ($FORM{$name}) {
              $FORM{$name} .= " $value";
        }
        else {
              $FORM{$name} = $value;
        }
}



#
# Write to Report File
#

append($REPORT);



#
# generic HTML page generator to provide feedback to users
#
#

print "Content-type: text/html\n\n";

print <<_END_OF_HTML;

<html>
<head>
<title> Instruction Survey Results </title>
</head>

<body bgcolor="#CCCC66">

<center>
<h2>University of LITA Libraries</h2>
<hr>
<h3>Instruction Survey Results</h3>

Thank You for taking our survey.
<br>
We hope your input will help us provide better services to the LITA
community.

<br>
<br>
```

```
<b>$FORM{'first'}</b>, you are a winner!

<br>
<br>
<a href="http://www.lita.org">Back to the LITA Homepage!</a>

<br><br><br>
$TIMESTAMP
<br>
<hr>


</body>
</html>

_END_OF_HTML

exit(1);



#
# append module is designed to be passed a path and filename; it
appends
# the form data to a comma delimited file
#

sub append {
	($FILE) = @_;		# puts the value we sent it ($REPORT_QUIZ)
into $FILE

	open ( APPEND_FILE, ">>" . $FILE ) || opendie($FILE);
#	flock (APPEND_FILE, $EXCLUSIVE_LOCK);
	@fields =
("last","first","student","before","frequency","evaluation");
# the fields you will use (except for the very last one), using the
names
# and the order they will appear in your database table
	foreach $field (@fields) {
		$fresh = $FORM{$field};
		$fresh =~ s/,//g;
		$fresh =~ s/"//g;
		print APPEND_FILE "\"$fresh\",";	# all but last
question
	}
	$fresh = $FORM{'comments'};		# the very last field in our
database
	$fresh =~ s/,//g;
	$fresh =~ s/"//g;
	print APPEND_FILE "\"$fresh\"";		# no comma after last
question
	print APPEND_FILE "\n";		# new line (like pressing enter)

#	flock (APPEND_FILE, $UNLOCK);
	close (APPEND_FILE);
}
```

A3. Comma-Delimited Text File

```
"doe", "jane", "yes", "books", "3", "4"
"smith", "ted", "no", "books journals", "2", "2"
```

A4. Faculty Research Example

```
<HTML>
<HEAD>
<TITLE>Faculty Research - Print vs. Online</TITLE>
</HEAD>
<BODY>
<CENTER>
<H3>Faculty Survey Form</H3>
<H4>Print vs. Online Resources</H4>
<small>Comments to:  <a
href="mailto:bogus@uiuc.edu.com">bogus@uiuc.edu.com</a>
<hr>
</CENTER>
Please answer the questions below about your library's decisions
regarding purchasing multiple formats of materials.  Results
will be posted soon!
<br>
<br>
<FORM ACTION="/cgi-bin/my_script.pl" METHOD="post">
<ul>
<li>Type of Library: Public<INPUT TYPE="radio" NAME="type"
VALUE="public">
School<INPUT TYPE="radio" NAME="type" VALUE="school">
University/Academic<INPUT TYPE="radio" NAME="type" VALUE="univ">

<li>Acquisitions Budget (Approx.):
<SELECT NAME="budget">
    <option value="1">$0 - $10,000
    <option value="2">$10,001 - $50,000
      <option value="3">$50,001 - $200,000
      <option value="4">Over $200,000
</select>

<li>Check which format your policy is to collect for reference books:
<INPUT TYPE="radio" NAME="ref" VALUE="paper">Paper
<INPUT TYPE="radio" NAME="ref" VALUE="online">Online
<INPUT TYPE="radio" NAME="ref" VALUE="both">Both
<INPUT TYPE="radio" NAME="ref" VALUE="depends">Depends

<li>Check all formats you collect for serials:
<INPUT TYPE="checkbox" NAME="serial" VALUE="paper">Paper
<INPUT TYPE="checkbox" NAME="serial" VALUE="online">Online
<INPUT TYPE="checkbox" NAME="serial" VALUE="microfiche">Microfiche

</ul>
Please share your experiences and decisions regarding multiple format
purchasing:
<br>
<TEXTAREA NAME="comments" VALUE="" COLS="40" ROWS="5"></TEXTAREA>
<br>
<INPUT TYPE="reset" VALUE="reset the form!">
<br>
<INPUT TYPE="submit" VALUE="Submit the Form">

</FORM>
<hr>
</BODY>
</HTML>
```

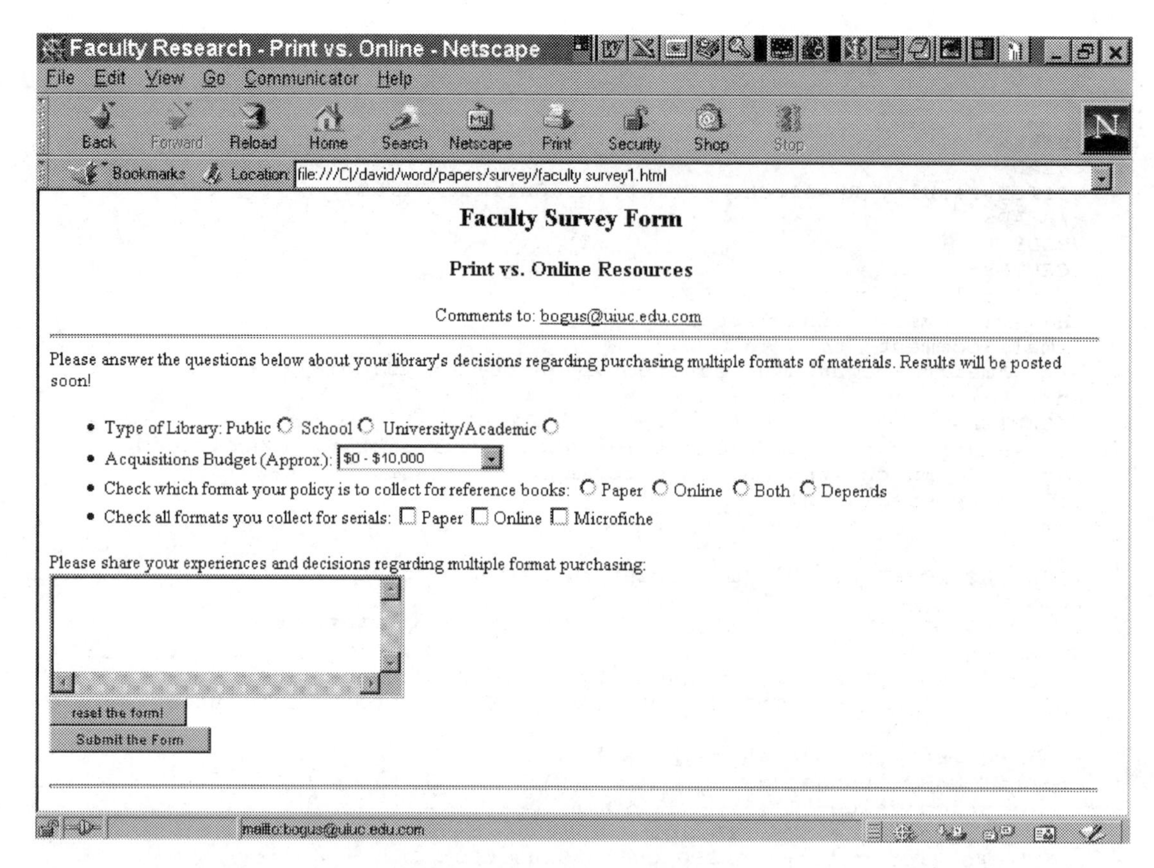

Screenshot of Faculty Research Survey

A5. Student Internet Use Survey Example

```
<HTML>
<HEAD>
<TITLE>Unliversity of LITA Library Internet Use Survey</TITLE>
</HEAD>
<BODY>
<CENTER>
<H3>Unliversity of LITA Library Internet Use Survey</H3>
<img src="lita logo.jpg" width="50" height="50" border="0" alt="Lita
Logo" align="middle">
Take it now and win cash prizes!<hr>
</CENTER>
<small>
<FORM ACTION="/cgi-bin/my_script.pl" METHOD="post">
What is your student status?
<select multiple name="year" size=2>
    <option value="fresh" selected>Freshman
    <option value="soph">Sophomore
      <option value="jun">Junior
      <option value="sen">Senior
      <option value="grad">Graduate Student
      <option value="not">Not a Student
</select>
<br>

How often do you use the Internet for researching a paper?
<SELECT  NAME="frequency">
<OPTION VALUE=4>Always
<OPTION VALUE=3 selected>Most of the Time
<OPTION VALUE=2>Occasionally
<OPTION VALUE=1>Never
</SELECT>
<br>
How Confident are you at finding what you need on the Internet?
<br>
<INPUT TYPE="radio" NAME="find" VALUE="4">Very Confident
<INPUT TYPE="radio" NAME="find" VALUE="3">Somewhat Confident
<INPUT TYPE="radio" NAME="find" VALUE="2">Not Very Confident
<INPUT TYPE="radio" NAME="find" VALUE="1">Lost
</SELECT>
<br>
What Website do you use to search the Net?<INPUT TYPE="text"
NAME="search" VALUE="">
<br>
Describe When you search the Internet, and How you search it:
<br>
<TEXTAREA NAME="comments" VALUE="" COLS="40" ROWS="5"></TEXTAREA>
<br>
<INPUT TYPE="reset" VALUE="reset the form!">
<br>
<INPUT TYPE="submit" VALUE="Submit the Form">

</FORM>
<hr>
</BODY>
</HTML>
```

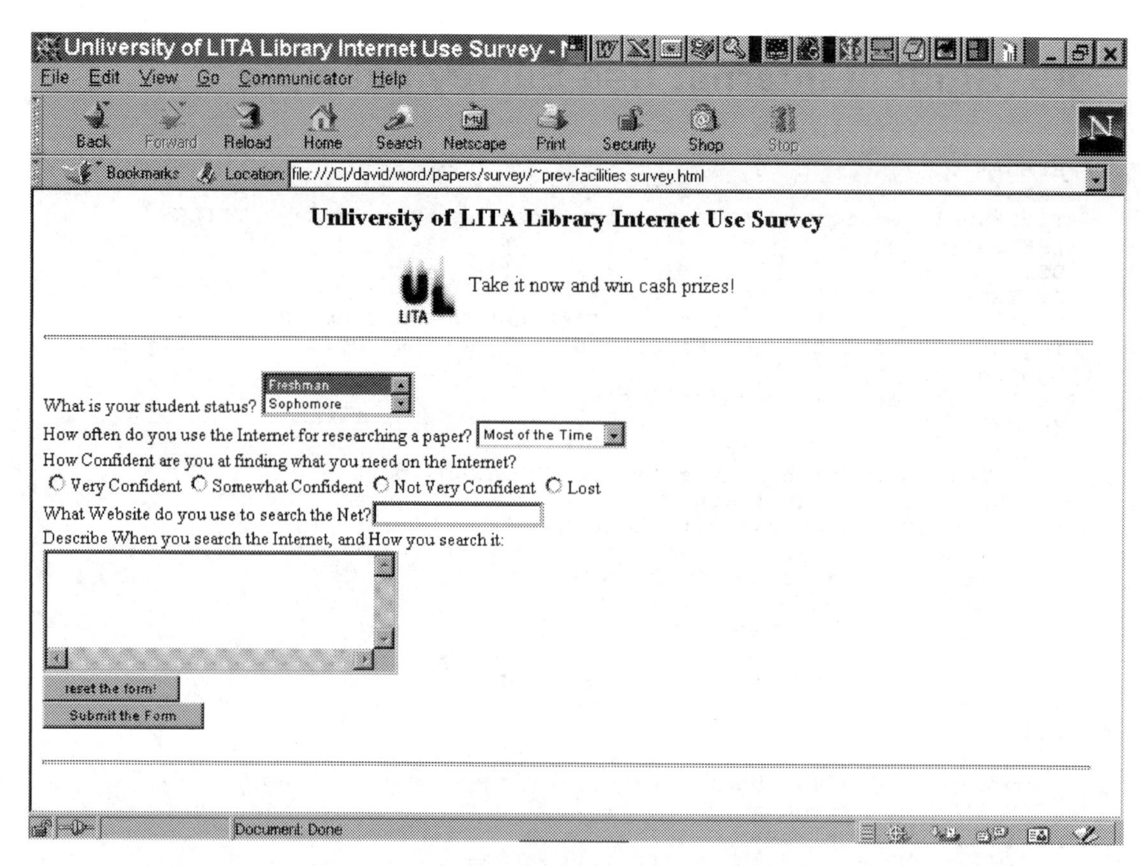

Screenshot of Internet Use Survey

A6. Reference Use Survey Example

```
<HTML>
<HEAD>
<TITLE>Unliversity of LITA Library Reference Survey</TITLE>
</HEAD>
<BODY> <CENTER>
<H3>Unliversity of LITA Library Reference Survey</H3>
<img src="lita logo.jpg" width="50" height="50" border="0" alt="Lita
Logo" align="middle">
Take it now and win cash prizes!<hr>
</CENTER>
<small>
<FORM ACTION="/cgi-bin/my_script.pl" METHOD="post">
What is your student status?
<select multiple name="year" size=2>
    <option value="fresh" selected>Freshman
    <option value="soph">Sophomore
      <option value="jun">Junior
      <option value="sen">Senior
      <option value="grad">Graduate Student
      <option value="not">Not a Student
</select>
<br>
How often do you use ask for help at the Library?
<SELECT  NAME="frequency">
<OPTION VALUE=4>Always
<OPTION VALUE=3 selected>Most of the Time
<OPTION VALUE=2>Occasionally
<OPTION VALUE=1>Never
</SELECT>
<br>
Who do you use ask for help at the Library?
<SELECT  NAME="ask">
<OPTION VALUE=4>Librarian
<OPTION VALUE=3>Regular Staff
<OPTION VALUE=2 selected>Friend
<OPTION VALUE=1>Other Students
<OPTION VALUE=0>Don't Ask Anyone
</SELECT>
<br>
What would you like to know more about?
<br>
<INPUT TYPE="radio" NAME="help" VALUE="research">Finding Books and
Articles
<INPUT TYPE="radio" NAME="help" VALUE="direction">Locating things
within the Library
<INPUT TYPE="radio" NAME="help" VALUE="computers">Using the Computers
<INPUT TYPE="radio" NAME="help" VALUE="paper">Writing my paper
<br>
Describe a typical conversation you have had with a library employee:
<br>
<TEXTAREA NAME="comments" VALUE="" COLS="40" ROWS="5"></TEXTAREA>
<br>
<INPUT TYPE="reset" VALUE="reset the form!">
<br>
<INPUT TYPE="submit" VALUE="Submit the Form">
</FORM>
<hr>
</BODY>
</HTML>
```

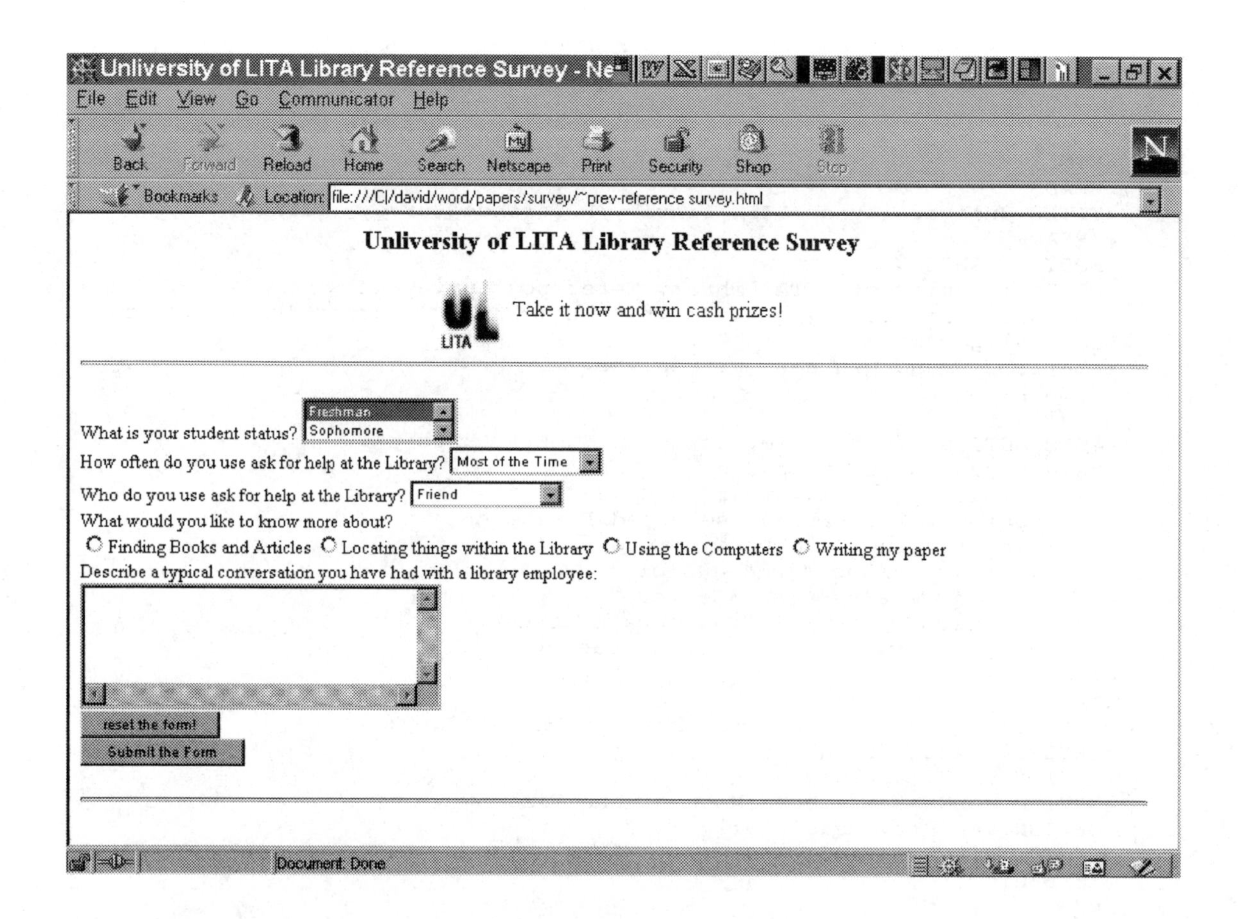

Screenshot of Reference Use Survey

A7. W3C Accessibility Guidelines Compliant Example

(see the W3C's page http://www.w3.org/TR/WAI-WEBCONTENT-TECHS/#forms for full details on the HTML tags used below)

```
<HTML>
<HEAD>
<TITLE>Sample ADA Compliant HTML Form</TITLE>
</HEAD>
<BODY>
<CENTER>
<H3>University of LITA Library Survey Form</H3>
Take it now and win cash prizes!
<hr>
</CENTER>
<FORM ACTION="/cgi-bin/my_script.pl" METHOD="post">
<FIELDSET>
<LEGEND>Personal Information</LEGEND>
<br>
<LABEL for="last">Last Name:</LABEL><INPUT TYPE="text" NAME="last"
VALUE="" tabindex="1">
<LABEL for="first">First Name:</LABEL><INPUT TYPE="text" NAME="first"
VALUE="" tabindex="2">
<br>
Are you a ULITA student?
<LABEL for="student">Yes</LABEL><INPUT TYPE="radio" NAME="student"
VALUE="yes" checked tabindex="3">
<LABLE for="student">No</LABEL><INPUT TYPE="radio" NAME="student"
VALUE="no" tabindex="4">
</FIELDSET>
<br><br>
<FIELDSET>
<LEGEND>Library Use Information</LEGEND>
<br>
<LABEL for="before">Check all the following you have used in the
library:</LABEL>
<INPUT TYPE="checkbox" NAME="before" VALUE="books" tabindex="5">Books
<INPUT TYPE="checkbox" NAME="before" VALUE="journals"
tabindex="6">Journals
<INPUT TYPE="checkbox" NAME="before" VALUE="online"
tabindex="7">Online Resources
<INPUT TYPE="checkbox" NAME="before" VALUE="staff" tabindex="8">Staff
<br>
<LABEL for="frequency">I come to the library:</LABEL>
<SELECT multiple NAME="frequency" size="2" tabindex="9">
<OPTION VALUE=4>More than once a week
<OPTION VALUE=3 selected>Weekly
<OPTION VALUE=2>Monthly
<OPTION VALUE=1>Less than Monthly
</SELECT>
<br>
<LABEL for="evaluation">I think overall the library is:</LABEL>
<SELECT NAME="evaluation" tabindex="10">
<OPTION VALUE=4>Very Useful
<OPTION VALUE=3>Somewhat Useful
<OPTION VALUE=2>Not Useful
<OPTION VALUE=1>Rather Watch TV
</SELECT>
<br>
```

```
<LABEL for="comments">Comments:</LABEL>
<br>
<TEXTAREA NAME="comments" VALUE="Enter Comments Here!" COLS="40"
ROWS="5" tabindex="11"></TEXTAREA>
<br>
</FIELDSET>
<INPUT TYPE="reset" VALUE="reset the form!" tabindex="12">
<br>
<INPUT TYPE="submit" VALUE="Submit the Form" tabindex="13">

</FORM>
<hr>
</BODY>
</HTML>
```

Sample ADA Compliant HTML Form - Netscap
File Edit View Go Communicator Help
University of LITA Library Survey Form
Take it now and win cash prizes!
Personal Information
Last Name: First Name:
Are you a ULITA student? Yes No
Library Use Information
Check all the following you have used in the library: Books Journals Online Resources Staff
More than once a week
I come to the library: Weekly
I think overall the library is: Very Useful
Comments:
reset the form!
Submit the Form
Document: Done

Screenshot of W3C Accessibility Compliant HTML FORM

A8. Importing a File Into Microsoft EXCEL

The procedure for this is very similar to what we did with Access. Unlike Access, however, with excel you don't need to do as much setup work – creating tables, forms, etc. Excel will let you open your comma-delimited file like a regular document. Headings, separators, graphs, etc. can all be added in later.

First, open the text file by choosing File>>Open. Change the "Files of Type" box in the lower left to "Text Files," then go to the directory containing your comma-delimited file.

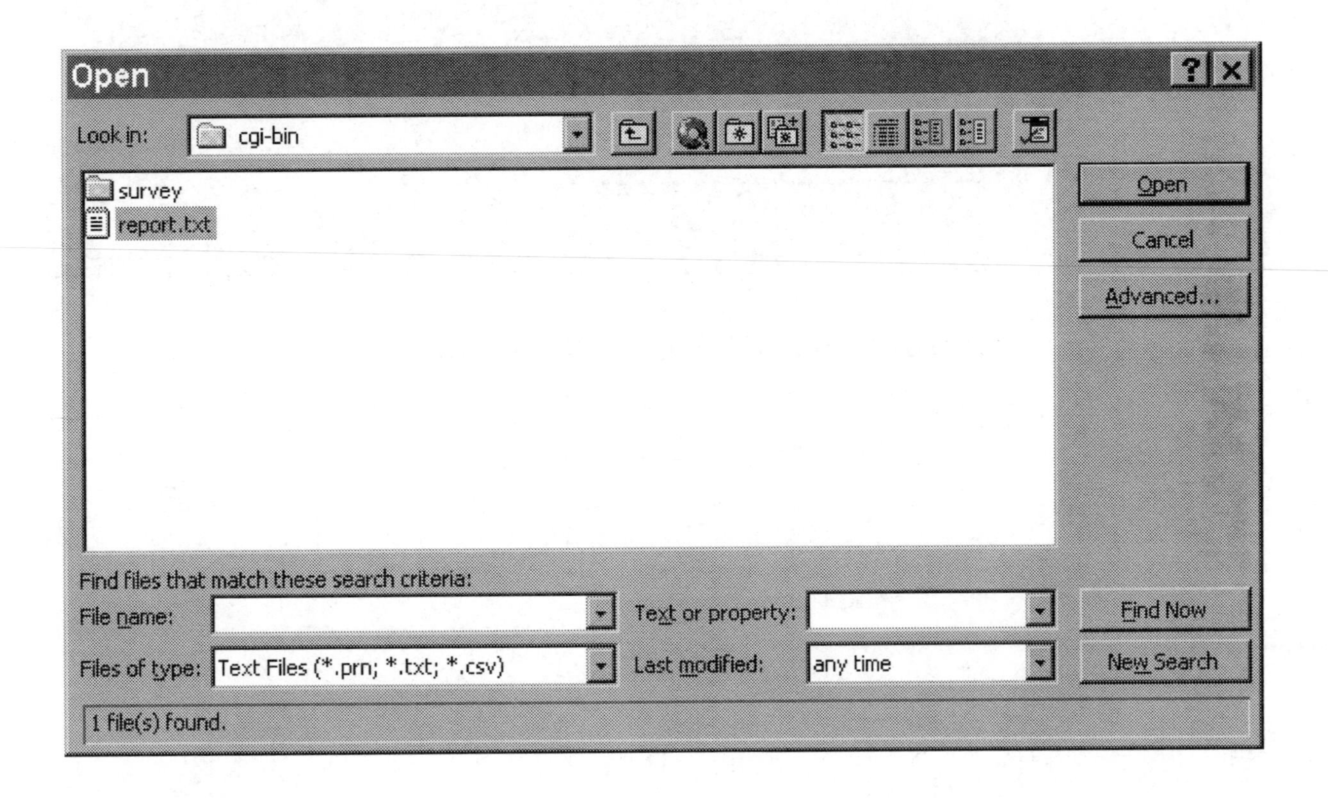

Screenshot of XCEL Open Dialog

The next dialog box will ask you if the data is delimited – this should be checked by default. Click Next.

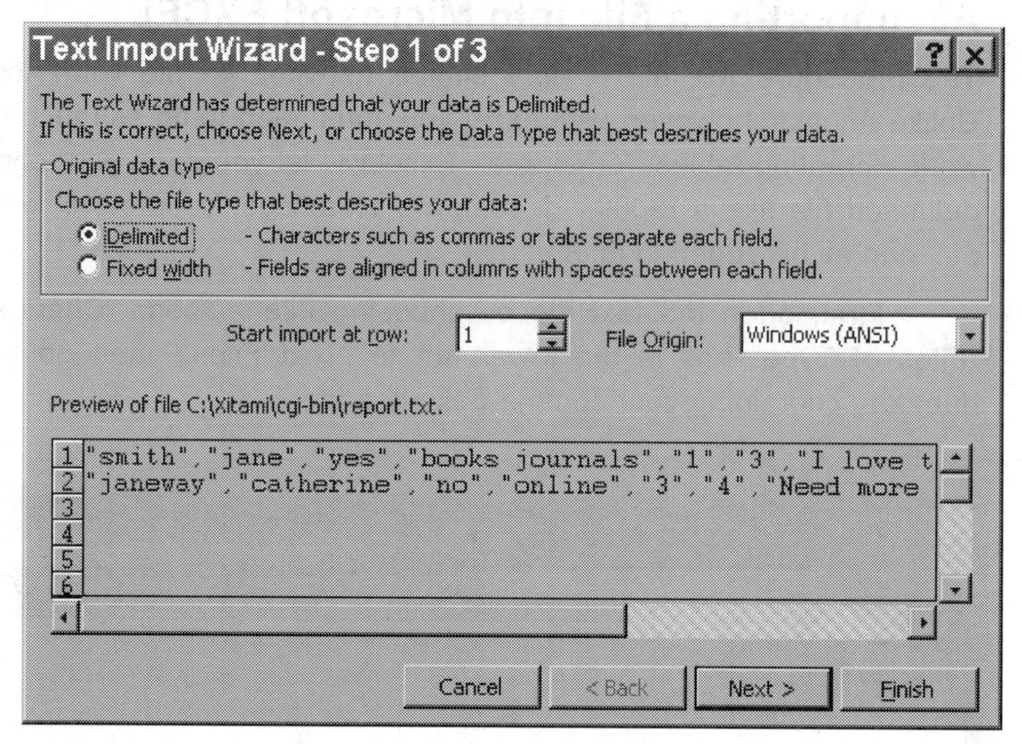

Screenshot of XCEL Import Wizard, Step 1

In the next dialog, choose "Comma" for your delimiter, and make sure the double quote (") is selected as the "Text Qualifier."

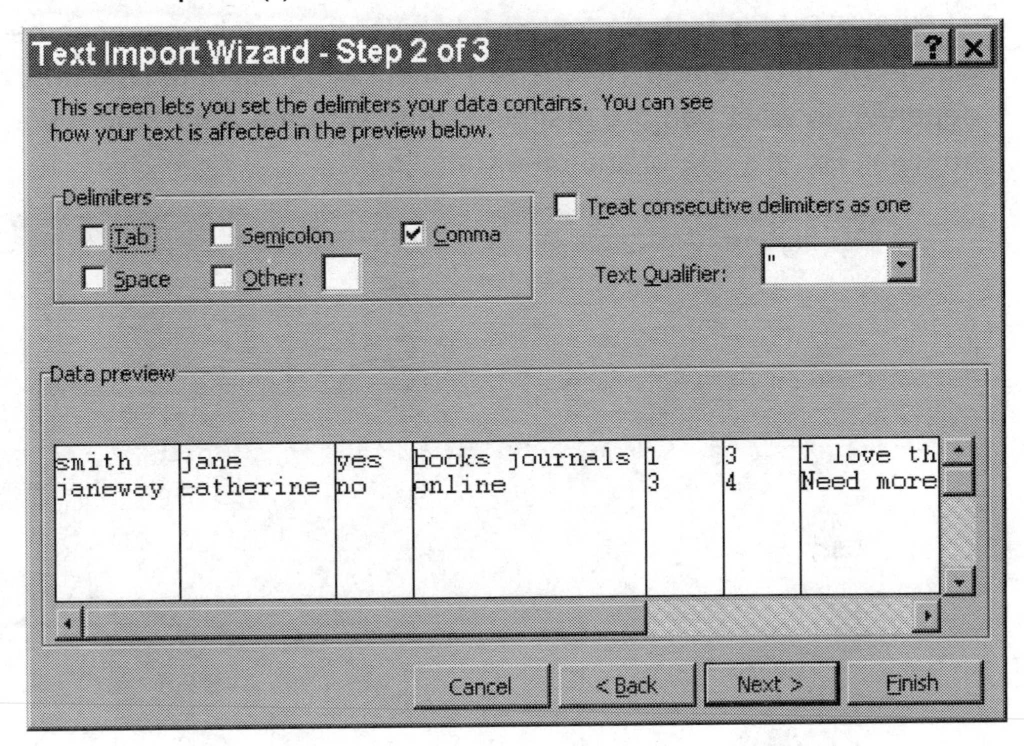

Screenshot of XCEL Import Wizard, Step 2

Finally, Excel will ask you if you want to format each column – this is the same as Access in Table Design mode, where you choose whether a field is text, a number, etc. You can make changes here, or just leave the default ("General") checked. Making changes really depends on what you are planning to do with the data, and if you plan on using Excel's charts and other functions.

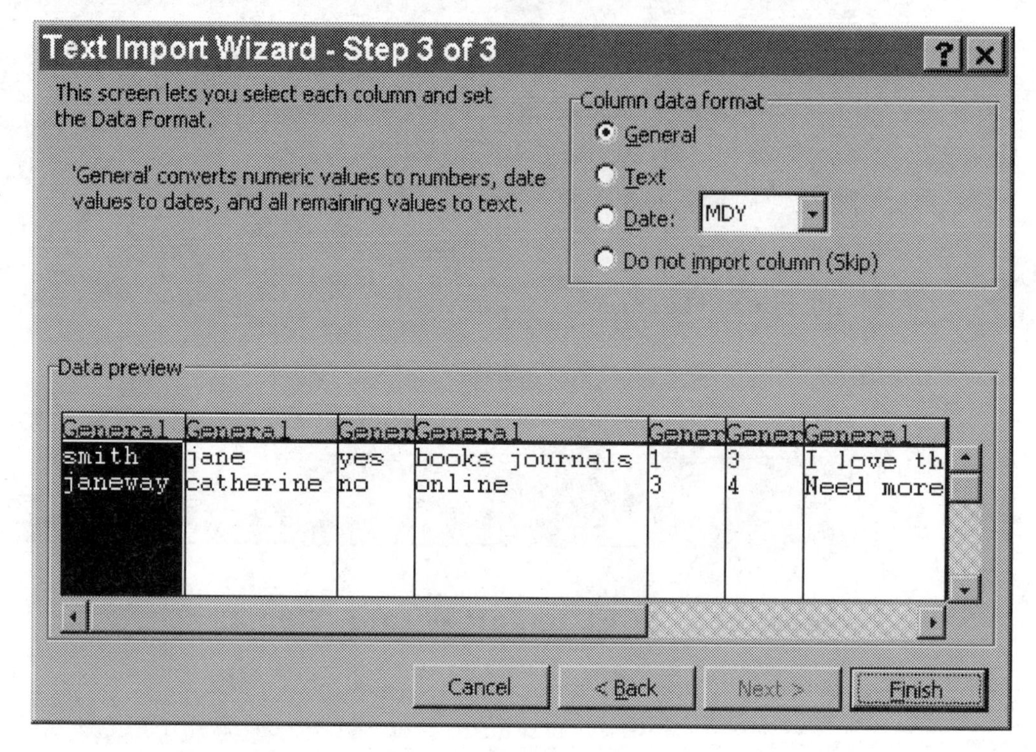

Screenshot of Excel Import Wizard – Step 3

Here is what the final result looks like. At this point, column headers, data calculations, etc. can be made.

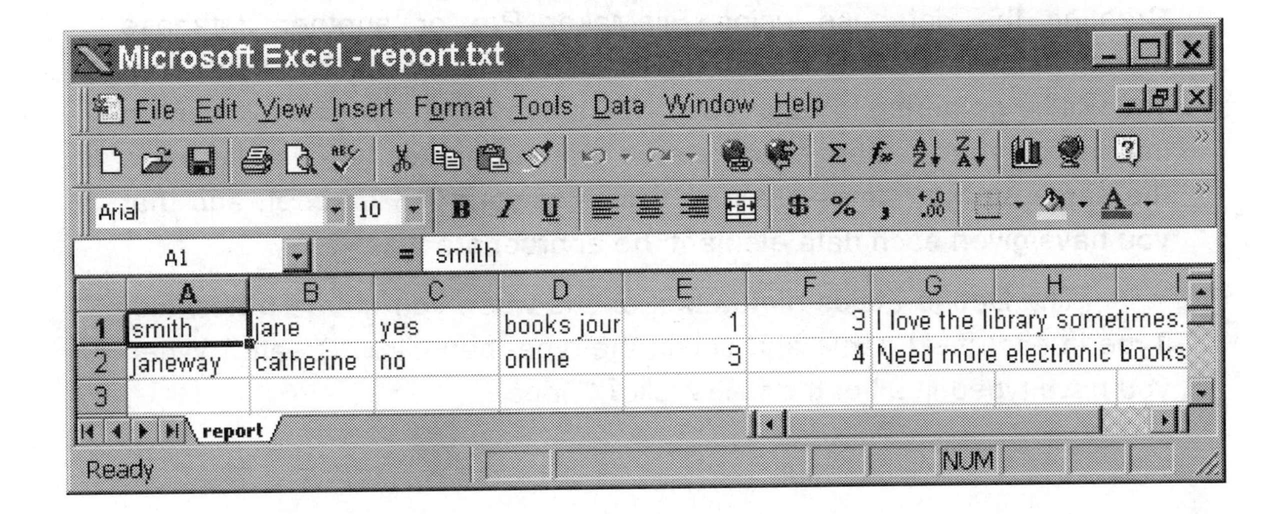

Screenshot of XCEL Spreadsheet after Importing

A9. Creating a Database Using FileMaker Pro

Creating the database using FileMaker Pro or another database management system is quite simple. First, you define the fields that you will be gathering through your Web survey and that you will want to import into your database. Make sure that the names you use here are the same as the names given to values in your PERL script, and that you have given each data element the appropriate type.

The Define Fields dialog box opens when you create a new file. Type in each field name and select the type then click "Create." When you have typed in all of the fields, click "Done."

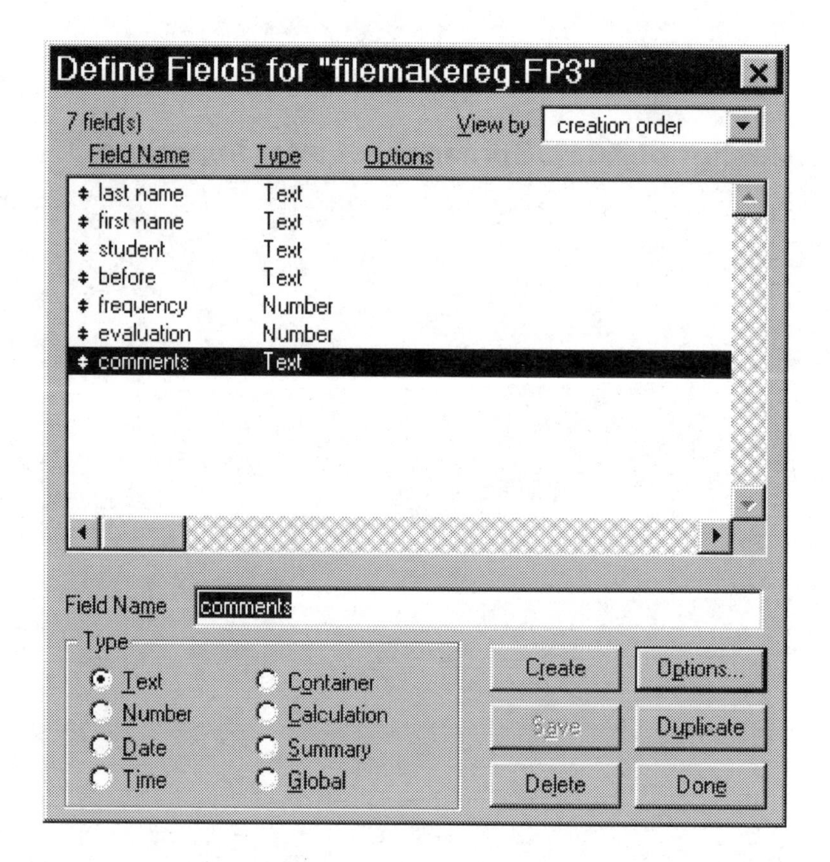

Screenshot of FileMaker Define Fields box

Here's the FileMaker Pro layout view for our database. This screen displays automatically after you click "Done" from the Define Fields dialog.

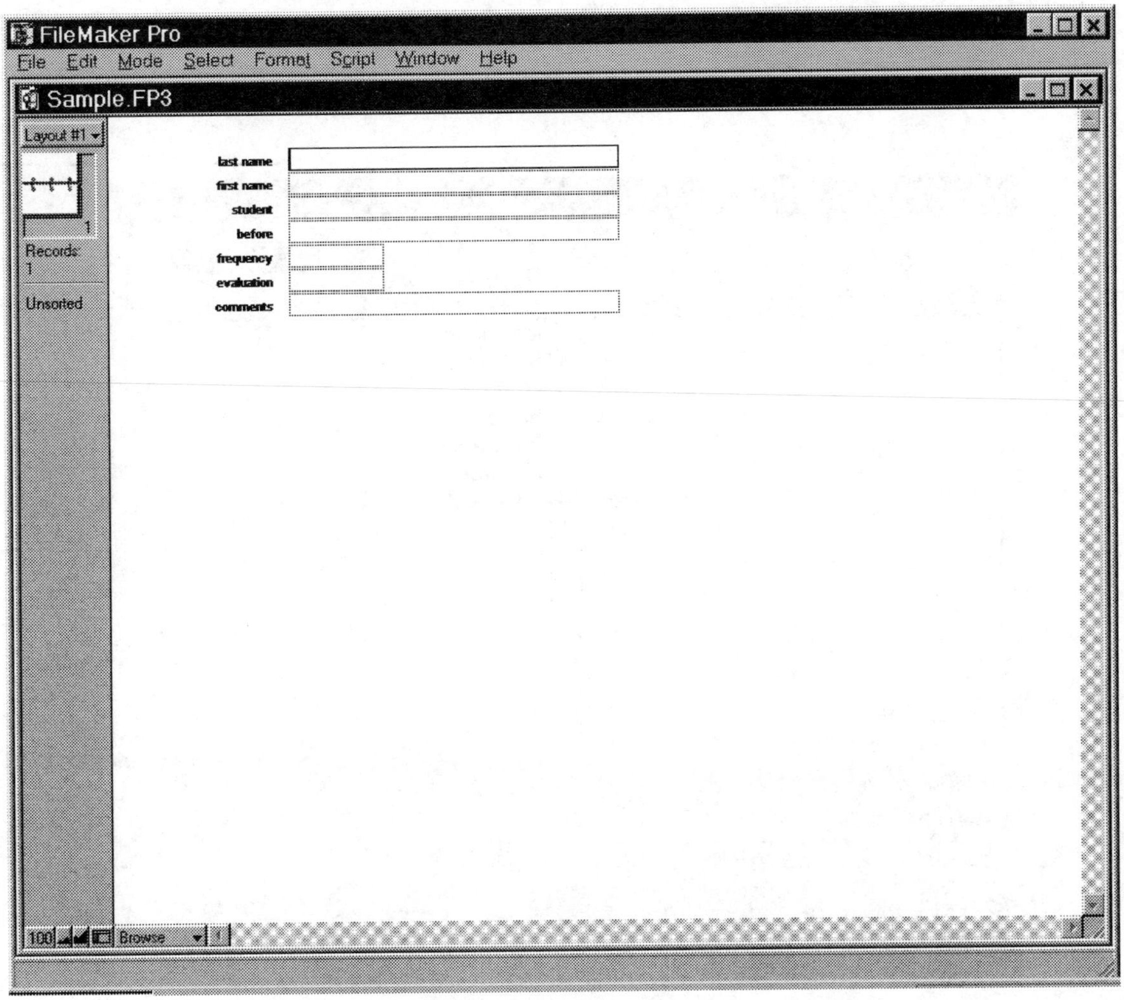

Screenshot of FileMaker Layout View

Like most database management systems, Filemaker Pro has an import function that easily recognizes the comma-delimited file format that we have produced as output from our survey. Click File/Import-Export/Import Records. Locate the file created by your PERL script and click "Open." You will see the first record and the corresponding FileMaker fields that the data will be imported to. If this is correct, click "Import." If it isn't correct (i.e. if there are more fields on one side of the dialog than on the other) then you will need to return to the Define Fields dialog and fix your fields list. Remember, you need a FileMaker field for every field you output from your survey.

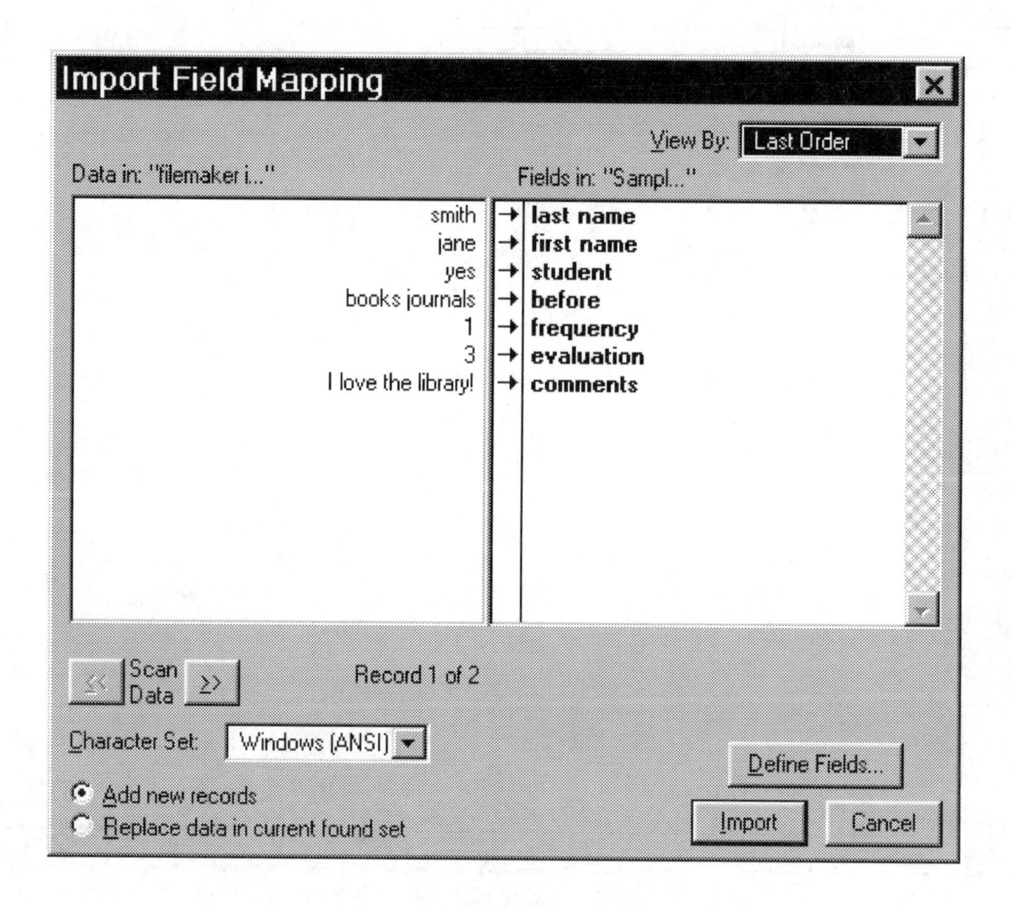

Screenshot of FileMaker Import Dialog Box

The data in the imported file can now be viewed and processed as any regular FileMaker Pro dataset. This is the Preview view that allows you to view the file as it would look when printed.

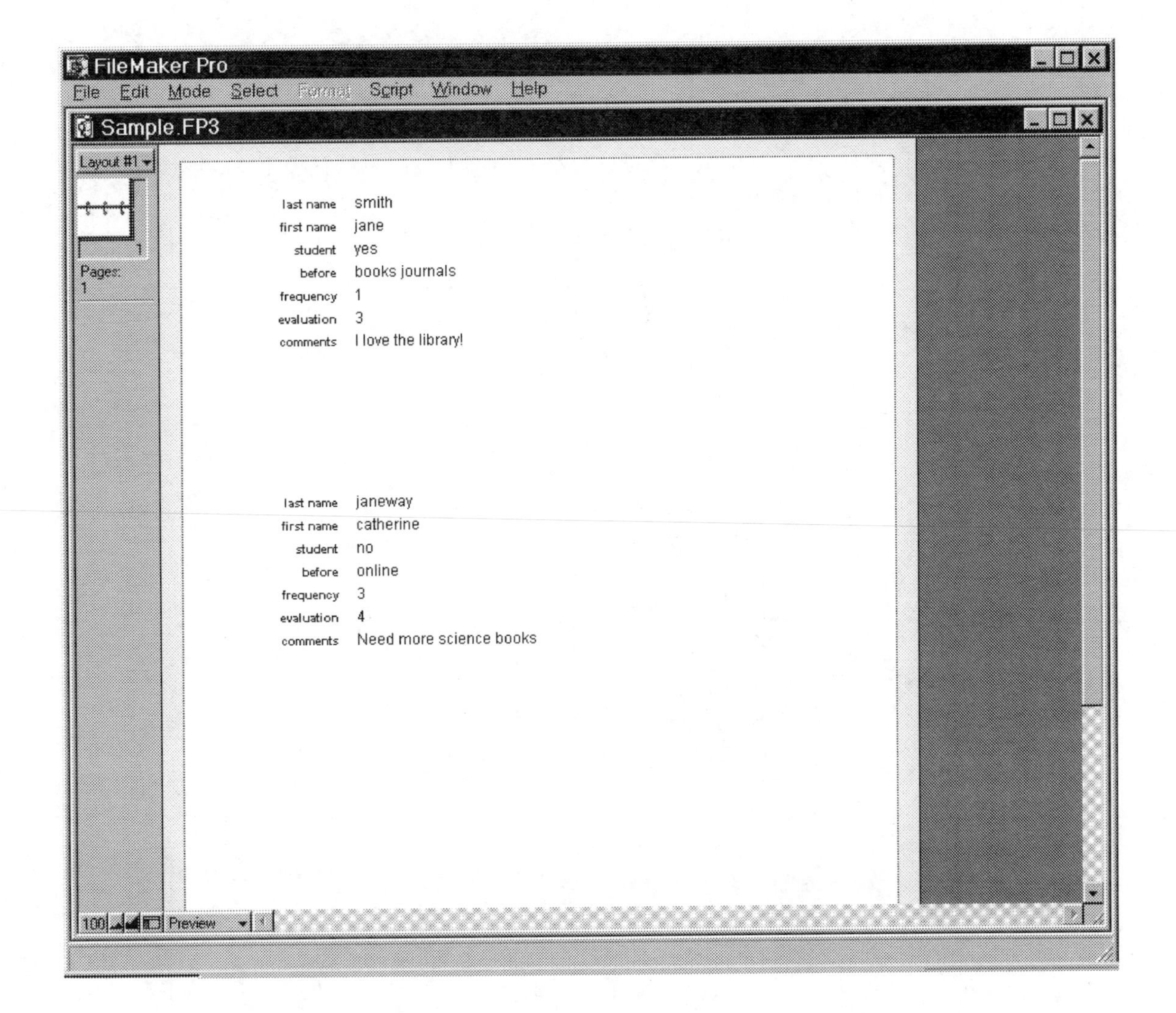

Screenshot of FileMaker Preview View